Love
Lived
Too
Long

Scott Shaw

Buddha Rose Publications

Loved Lived Too Long
Copyright © 1987 by Scott Shaw
All Rights Reserved

Cover Painting by Scott Shaw
Rear Cover Photograph of Scott Shaw
By Hae Won Shin
Copyright © All Rights Reserved

1st Edition 1988
2nd Edition 2016

ISBN 10:1-877792-21-7
ISBN 13: 9781877792212

Library of Congress Control Number:
2016953708

10 9 8 7 6 5 4 3 2 1

Printed in the United States of America

Love
Lived
Too
Long

Introduction

About a year and a half ago, the girl these pages were written about and I sat in this Nuevo-High Tech Shopping Mall, eating Big Macs and drinking cappuccino. *"How poetic,"* I thought. We were discussing my potential move to the apartment building I currently inhabit and am writing in right now. This building, right here, right up against the Pacific Ocean. The sound of the waves crash in my ears. It was then/it was there that I began to consider writing the story of her and I. It was also at that point that the title, *"Love Lived Too Long,"* came to me.

But, as I have been complying these words over the past several months I have realized that it would be virtually impossible to ever put our story to pen; all the ups and all the downs and the roundabouts. As well as it would do my already faltering reputation as a decent and sane individual no good whatsoever if I were to reveal all the mistreatment I put her, (the woman these pages are about), through. It is for this reason that I have attached the aforementioned title to this work. I will leave our full-blown story left to those who have the unique gift and the means to access the akashic records.

In terms of historical perspective, it is important to note that though I have written poetry and song ever since I was very young, it was not until my mid twenties that I became what may be termed, *"An autobiographical poet."* For this reason, most of this work was taken from a period post our first few years together, as prior to that I wrote in much different/more abstract style. A style that would probably give no credence to our actual life/time that was spent together.

These words, they are my words; if the story were to be told by her, (in all due respect), I am sure there would be a much different storyline presented. Read on…

ॐ

S.
88.29.6
Redondo Beach, California

Forward

Have you ever had one of those loves that goes on for ever and ever; ever and ever to nowhere? This was my case/this was our case: hers and mine. Seven years, a long time...

These are some of the words which I wrote for her/about her/inspired by her; my long time seven-year love.

Though the truth be told, there were millions more words, scribbled upon the pages of my creative journals, that can/could be attributed to her and the feelings and emotions that she evoked. But, maybe those writings will be uncovered another day or maybe not? I do not know...

But here, these are some of the feelings, turned into words: the ups and the downs, the feel goods and the feel bads, the loves and the hates. Feelings, felt/life lived - lived between here and I.

She meant so much to me, she became such an integral part of my life; there was so much attachment, that though I tried, time-and-time again, to walk away/run away; freeing myself from her grasp/spell, for whatever reason, it/that became all but impossible.

In fact, leaving her... Had I been half the man that I could have been I would have never even tried/would never have even thought about it, and we would have lived, as in all the story books, *happily ever after*. But, if that had been

the case, then/there would not be all
this poetry.

So, here you go… Here's some of the
written stuff that maybe you can relate
to? Or, maybe not? Stuff I wrote,
inspired by/because of her.

The Words

1.

has peace risen in the winds of love
or was it just a rap
that went too far

from the source of a club
where I don't think ladies should be
to meet a lady
a real lady
spent the night
the first night

with love always a predominate
longing in my mind
to search
is to never find
to give up the search
to live together
we move so soon
we move so fast
we are
we come

she is
a little/a lot too raggy
a little/a lot too spacey
yeah, she is selfish

why did we start

the answer lies
in that we started too soon

looking for something that wasn't there

has peace risen in the wind of love?

2.

rainy day in january
and things are going slow
sitting back
playing music
and trying to feel
the way I felt
so long ago

morning songs
of the rain
ringing through my ears
morning love
through the evening
taken me through
until it's time to leave

and the time is growing near

time to leave
leaving soon
and the time is growing near
trying to leave
trying to love
soon to realize that the love
is already here

trees with no leaves
touching the sky
love that should never have been
taking it through
another mystic night time

the rain
washing away
all the pain that is here
with it comes the new sun
showing me that my time to leave
is drawing near

time to leave
leaving soon
and the time is already here
trying to leave
trying to love
soon to realize
that true love
is so near

3.

shower in the moon light
our love, where did it go
magic turns to mystery
as we watch the night time flow

the love
where did it come from
leaving
only to find that there is nowhere else
to go
fantasies and memories
sitting on the roof
the light in the sky
takes us through
to another memory
that will not leave us alone

the place
my place
was it ever there
the space
my space
nothing left
where did it go

where has our time gone

one too many disagreements
one too many loves
one too many night times spent together
when all there was
was a place to roll over

yes, I love you
yes, I know that you love me
artist to artist

poet to poet
is there anything left
that needs to be done

reaching new summits
but is it one
where we will only fall off
dancing to new rhythms
is there any way to turn it down

love in the leisure
continuing the way it is
moments held down by procedure
where is there left to go

4.

hello my spanish love
how we hate each other
how we love each other
how we beat each other up
how we feel suicidal
due to each other
and how we long to be away
from each other
why?

each day I desire to
no longer be with you
each day passes by
each day, even though
they are not appreciated
I buy you all your dreams
all except
the love that you want from me
the type
which I cannot give

I don't know
are we too much alike?

but ah
how I love
oriental eyes
(even if they don't have eyelids
as you have pointed out
and they wear make up
to cover this fact up)

and ah
how I love momentary fantasies

ah
how I love
these things

why than
is it you
who I always call

5.

just received
a telephone call from her

"Why are you being icky," she asks.
"Not icky," I answer,
"Just a little sad."

6.

trapped
under the cage
of her
my L.A. woman/spanish love
one more week
has gone by
two weeks
since my return
two weeks home
one month the equal
the expectations
I have had
the desires
still un-lived
two weeks
I have been home
how I hope
I do not die a man
desires and dreams
unfulfilled
another week
has passed
under the cage
of her
perhaps she writes
another week
gone by
under the cage
of me

what to do?

7.

I do not need to hear
too many more
I love yous
I do not need to
make love with you
all that often
all I need
is an occasional
cappuccino and croissant breakfast
and to know
that all I have given you
and done for you
has not been
a complete waste

8.

girl-a-holic

alcoholic
no
but
girl-a-holic
yes

does her presence cause me problems
yes
do I need her in the morning
yes
have I missed work due to her
        (well I have never had a job)
but similar creative stuff
yes
do I want her when I am alone
yes
has having her caused me financial
problems
yes
and all the other stuff
yes
yes
yes
yes
yes...

alcoholic
no
girl-a-holic
yes

9.

```
I'm sorry
please don't kill yourself
it is just
that the motionless pain
has gotten too strong
I can't take it
can't take it anymore
```

10.

thank you
for the gift of
suicidal tendency

I met you
you wanted to kill yourself
I lived with you
you wanted to kill yourself
I left you
you wanted to kill yourself

and now here I am
pointing a gun
to my own head
tying the noose
around my own neck

thank you
for the gift of
suicidal tendency

11.

a woman
who is my addiction
why do I always call her
I don't want to
why do I always spend money on her
I don't want to
why do I take her
always along
I don't want to
take her out

her and I
it has gotten
all so stale
I seek a new love
a new romance
why can't I leave her alone

12.

said goodbye to her
one more time

now will I be free
will it be alright
now can I have the woman/women
of my dreams?

said goodbye to her
one more time

now is my time
my own
will she check up on me?

said goodbye to her
one more time

now no one to waste my money
or all my time
no one to blame
am I free?

said goodbye to her
one more time

should I call her?
no, I must be strong

13.

entertainment for the neighbors
the yells and the screams
of our fights
why do I have a girl friend
who loves to raise her voice
screams and yells
as they listen
from upstairs
as they listen
from next door
it is none of their fucking business

entertainment for the neighbors
I wish I lived in a house

14.

mom
mom
mommy
mommy
I didn't do anything
don't hit me
please
mommy
mommy
as she speaks
all I can do is listen
pop
pop
poppy
poppy
she speaks in spanish
I cannot understand
as she cries herself
into a cathartic, catatonic state
due to the wounds
which I have inflicted
mommy
mommy
poppy
poppy
for an hour or more
she lays there as she hyperventilates
her tears
I began to cry too
for her
because of the uncontrolled fool
which I am

for me
because I have no mommy or poppy
that I can cry to
mommy
mommy

poppy
poppy
all I can do
now that my damage is done
is hold her
rock her
pray that she can forgives me

and me
the low man
that I am to her
writes a poem about it
mommy
mommy
poppy
poppy

15.

my addiction
goes so deep
into the arms
of my latin love
who I hate
who I love to hate
who I love
who I hate to love
I long to be away from her
yet, I cannot go
I cannot kick the addiction
I need a substitution

worse than heroin
love kills

16.

the choice tonight
the walls
the T.V.
go out maybe
walk the strand alone
or
take out a woman
a woman who hates me
a woman who I hate
with whom the relationship
could get no worse
1 could look forward to
a upsetting evening
getting nothing done
except getting more upset
and hating every minute of it

either/or
sounds like a viable choice
guess I'll go out w/ her

17.

telephone
busy signal
rejection
of the worst kind
no, I will not speak to you
I'm too busy
I am speaking to someone else

18.

morning is dawning
on the horizon
as she lay next to me
I cum in my sleep
a fantasy
somewhere lived
somewhere fulfilled
it wakes her

a bad way to be woken
on this summer morning

19.

life without her

who will I call all the time
especially in the late hours
of the night?
who will I eat out with each evening?
who will I spend all my money on?
who will I complain to?
who will I blame for all that goes
wrong?
who will I take all my aggressions
out on?
who will I be
far stuck in the middle of love
and hate with?
who will I cheat on?
who will I fell pressure from
when ever I'm a minute late?
or not late at all
just pressure to be home
who will I confide in?
who will know me like
no one else knows me?
who will be my only artistic
inspiration?
and who will I cuddle up with all
through the night?

life without her

20.

writing letters to a babe in korea
while telephoning her
my L.A./spanish love
telling her that I miss her

"Don't lie to me," she says
"I never have lied to you, except about
women."

truth in a lie

our telephone conversation continues
we discuss
how there is no room
for a poet in this world

why should they
have to concern themselves with money
it should just be there for them

we talked of how ginsberg,
the publishing agent
made kerouac and burroughs

talking to her
while I feel the love shift
to my babe in korea

what can I say
what can I do
I love the freedom
I hate the loneliness

loving
shifting
from her

my L.A./spanish love
to korea
as I go
casually insane

21.

I speak to my mother
(my psychological enigma)
I explain to her
what do you do with people like her
    my L.A./spanish love
        and I
people who see another vision
you only try to make them normal
    have a job
    erase their vision
vision, however, cannot be erased
so there are those
I am one
visionary
who does not know how to cope
who does not know what to do

what do you suggest
send me to a psychiatrist
no
get me a job
no
so I, as others
like her,
my L.A./spanish love
sit in perpetual artistic
mystic
hell
    sounds so poetic
    it is not

22.

two nights ago
spiritual initiation night
she called me twice
twice from spain
5:00 P.M.
7:00 P.M.
somehow
the phone...
I had accidently disconnected it

she calls 9:00 A.M.
the next morning
I am out
    out already
far earlier than I normally rise
talking the bus
to Hollywood
to pick up my being repaired
automobile/porsche 356 sc

"Fuck you!"
it is on my telephone answering machine
*"Don't bother calling or coming here to
be with me."*

I call
we fight
1:00 A.M.
the next day
I call
we fight some more

than it is worked out
than it is explained
but I wonder
why
god laid it on me this time

perhaps
to free myself
for further adventures
perhaps
my lying karma
catching up with me
I do not know
but the truth does battle to come out
lies they are hard to hide
I must turn my life around
now is the time
now is the sign
no more lies
to my L.A. love
who is currently residing in spain

23.

go to europe
and visit her
my L.A./spanish love
go on through/past
on to india, nepal, sri lanka
than on to korea
to visit my awaiting korean love
than leave
leave them all behind
for japan
tokyo-kyoto-tokyo

vision
perhaps
vision
perhaps
not

than come home
new I hope
having stepped over the edge
one more time
maybe come home
the same
I do not know

new love, maybe
new vision, maybe
I do not know
time will tell
hard to explain
head trips

do this
don't do that
hard to explain
I do not know

24.

do you remember
the last night
that we slept together
in my loft apartment?

31 October - 1 November 1982
a long time ago

my van
it had broken down
we had taken it to the shop
to be fixed
we went
and rented
a brown rent-a-car
remember?

then, that night
with everything out of the apartment
we slept
upstairs
slept with one
sleeping bag
and our coats
to keep us
winter time warm
in the winter time cold
do you remember?

ah, memories
ah, love
I love you/I love the memories

25.

I know
that I only dig my grave further
speaking to her
my L.A./spanish love
on the expensive
international telephone lines

taking to her
sending her love letters
to a yet to be felt new love
living in korean form

out with
any woman
any chance to take another dance

with every dance
there is another chance

I am foolish
I don't know
right now
my mind goes to a taipei disco
a moment
a fantasy
lived four months ago
four months
it seems like forever

26.

I talk to my L.A./spanish love
on the international telephone
I know
she is just a spoiled brat
and I do mean brat

I am the one who has spoiled her
that is how I know

I do not long for her
no, not anymore
I do not even really want her
no, not any more
yet, I am addictive
yet, I am alone
I call her
she calls me
    collect
monthly telephone bills
of one thousands dollars or more
    that's just insane

soon I will go to spain
to visit her
while she attends art school
    for what purpose
    the answer
    in its addiction
    is no longer clear

to love?
to fuck?

to pay her way
to fly with me to italy
to france?
to listen to her bitch?

I do not know
I just do not know

yet, here in L.A.
I have no one
no one who understands me
it is so hard to find contact
with my kind of people
it is so hard

I speak to my current korean babe
she calls me collect too
collect again
collect from her homeland
almost every night
what a telephone bill to come
I hear her words
she loves me
and for a moment
I even love her
but I also know
women her age
her age and not married
not married
but who want to be
are a dime a dozen

looking for a man
any man
and love is easy to find
when
any man

any woman
will do
and it is easy to say
that you love them

love is easy
when anything will do

but for her to be here
be here in the states
I must throw away
all my dreams
I think death is better
what can I tell her
what can I say
how can I explain
I will not marry
a second best girl
for I know her story to come
I know all of her excuses

so I will spend
a few thousand dollars
visit her
kiss her

come to know her
leave her
en route home

and then there is this other babe
fairly local at least
in the abstract sense of the word
her english
it is not so good
her korean
not so bad

and her form
well, somewhere in between
her name it translates into
sweet, ruler

respectively
we had a night
last night
sixty dollars of dinner
sixty pounds of lust
and again tomorrow
we will go out
dinner, lust, and partial love
and now it is not
that I do not/did not
have my fantasies about her
but once they have been kissed
and the kiss
is only bloody
and not so sweet

what is left
only the desire
to find a way out

and I wonder why it is
in this world I don't meet people
that I can really relate to
people who I understand
people who understand me
I always meet
and am always left
with second best women
in a second best world

27.

I cannot
take her back now
her, my L.A./spanish love
there is
too much to hide

28.

melodrama to the maximum
lust
and love
hate and lies
we make love
we are in love
at least as far as it is possible
possible for her and I

she hangs up the telephone
hangs it up on me
I hang up the telephone
hang it up on her
a dreamed of new beginning
a longed for second chance
a passage
to the nothingness
but the phone
it will soon be redialed

the games of a child

and for a moment
there is hope
for a moment
there is a chance
hope
that it may be another way
a chance
that it will all be different
but in the end
there is only passion

the passion only held by love
the passion only known by hate
the action(s) taken only by the
engulfed

this intensity of passion
only experienced by a few
the poets
the artists
the dreamers
the visionaries

melodrama to the maximum

29.

my sins
keep me from you
my mind
my lust
makes me long
that you were here

30.

I call and talk to her
her, my L.A./spanish love
talk
on the telephone tonight
011-34-1-419-0663
madrid, espana
she tells me
I should go and have
a really good physical check-up
for I have been traveling
and partying way too long
way too hard
she tells me
I tell her
I do not want to go
because I am afraid of what
they will find

31.

yeah, it is just me
the one who is all alone
the one who wants
to drink coffee outside
on cool winter nights
wearing a tweed coat

it is just me
the one who dreams of
playing music
dreams of
art
poetry
mysticism
but who
because of lives
unfulfillment in other areas
slips on lives
painful banana peel

yeah, it is just me
who wants to go to europe now
japan next month
china and tibet in the fall
but who has to find
denied money
to make the journey

it is just me
who calls you in spain every night
simply so you can get mad
and hang up on me

it is just me
the one who longs for the feeling
of new love

but who is all alone

yeah, it is just me

32.

the phone rings
in the middle of the night
the middle of the night
the almost early morning
when I am finally asleep
international call
I hear
the international sound
"Hello."
no answer
disconnected
again
again
again
seven times
ten times
I don't know
same response
international disconnect

contact you to contact me
my L.A./spanish love
I am trying to
you are trying
an ocean
a continent
keeps us apart
you call
I call
all to no answer
international disconnect

I am alone
you are alone
just as I am learning
to be more tolerant of people
to be tolerant of life

this
and the ocean fog
coming in tonight
I wait
I want
to speak with you

and the sun begins
to light the sky

33.

a T.V. show
has brought me to tears tonight
not the show itself
but all the emotion in me
I look around
at guitars laying on the floor
of my messy apartment
eight years ago
I purchased some of them
eight years is a long time
I cry
I have no one to call
not even her
my L.A./spanish love
I don't even know where she is
I have no one
I just don't know
what to do in life
oh god
I don't know what to do
I sit here
I cry
I stare at guitars
laying on the floor
not making music
I know
many have more to cry about
than I
but still I cry
I don't know what to do
what direction to go
where to find the illusion

I cry
no one to even call
to say I'm crying
I sit here alone
very alone
and cry

34.

a bike ride
into the rain
into the 2:00 A.M. night
I come home
I see parked
in front of my apartment
an MG
once hers
now registered in my name
and for a moment
I wish she was waiting
for a moment
I wish she was home
arms
to fall in to
next saturday night
not to be spent alone
but we have parted
her to spain
I to the nights
alone
living in the moment
riding a bike
listening
meditating
in the rain
of a May
2:00 A.M. night
sing me your song

35.

now my uncle
gave me a thousand dollars today
      a birthday present
            cash
      I pined it up
      on my bulletin board

my mother
she gave me a hundred
I went to buy a book with it
but decided to put it back

my uncle said
he would give me a check
for three hundred more
"You have a bank account don't you?"
"Yes."
      I lied

now I could give this money
to my mother
to help her pay the bills
or I could go to spain
for a couple of weeks

I think I'll go to spain

shiftless
useless
irresponsible
etc.
etc.

I know
it kills me
as I live it
but death
in the arms of illusion
is far more valid
than death for no reason at all

36.

finish a conversation with,
"I'm dead tonight."
and I feel it

I come home
no messages
on the telephone answering machine
I'm safe
I'm free
she
my L.A./spanish love
didn't call tonight

but apparently she did
three times
she confronts me
I wasn't there to receive them
six thousand miles away
I'm busted
out fucking another meaningless babe

last week we talked
she called me a compulsive liar
I said I only lie to you about other
women
tonight she cries on the telephone
tell me
tell me
tell me the truth

and I lie
she was right
I am a compulsive liar
but just about women to other women

now/here

just when I am ready
and I see
that there is nothing happening

just then
between her and I
just when I see
that you don't meet
spiritual people
who know the wind
who feel it
in clubs
in discos
I am thrown away

I know my lies
and I know my desires
and I don't know what to do
I also know
that I don't want to hurt her
no
not
anymore

I always run back to her

me, I remember a hysterical promise
drunken/stoned
in tone and in mind
a promise
to god
as I walked
all alone on the strand
one manhattan beach night

"If she comes back to me
I won't fool around anymore."
"If she comes back to me
I will marry her."

I wonder now
how many people have lied to god

here I am
more than two years later
so alone
so wishing not to be
waiting
seeking
a new purpose
full of ideals
full of loneliness
and full of the knowledge
of what is the point
of being with someone
with no vision

where can I find
someone with vision

then, *"I'm dead tonight."*
but maybe
I already am
Maybe she is too
maybe
    at least
one step closer
maybe
for her and I
she is/I am

she and I
but, I hope not

my sad little girl
holding a doll
and wanting only love
only wanting love
and I the fool
caught in desires
of greener grasses
who leads her on
saying, *"I'm not a liar."*
as I lie

alone
dead tonight

37.

can I struggle
another ten minutes
waiting for the time to pass
waiting for the bars
of your permission
to be lifted
to call
to tell you
that I am home
I haven't gone out on you

may I take a walk down the beach
should I ride my bike
should I go and get a chef salad
in the late night restaurant
how can I be free

six thousand miles away bars
drawn by myself
I can't let her go
I don't want to be alone
yet, I seek
new romantic flavors

38.

"Did you paint a beautiful painting?"
"No, I don't paint beautiful
paintings."
"Did you paint an ugly painting?"
"No, I just stayed up all night
painting."
"Oh, is that why you are icky?"
"Yes, and you called too early."
"But it is past 12:00 A.M. here
so it is past 9:00 A.M. there."
"Yeah, but I'm tired and I stayed up
all night."
"Oh, sorry."

39.

it would be a lie
and worst of all
a lie to myself
if I said
I did not want to hold you again
if I said
I did not long to kiss you
make love with you again
it would be a lie
and I've told you
enough lies
saddened lies

today I get the feeling
I pick up the telephone
and I call
you answer
it has been a long time

a year since I last saw you
a year since I last loved you
a year spent sanely
or perhaps
a year wasted
perspective being the only judge

though I know
that we make each other crazy
I know we make each other mad
you spend my money
we spend our time
thrown into nothing

nothing of somethingness

it has been a long time

but it would be a lie
and worst of all
a lie to myself
if I said
I did not long to hold you again
if I said
I did not wish to kiss you
make love with you again
it would be a lie
and I've told you enough lies

40.

sitting
listening
waiting for her car to pull up
waiting for her to call
will she
I think not
at least
not until it is too late

sitting
listening
listening through the ears
of too many beers
beers drank all alone
when I once again
did not wish to be alone

41.

she looked at me
and said
you look good today
you look young
the stress that usually
shows in your face
is not there

42.

*"Could you come here and hug me
for a few minutes."
"Why?"
"Because I am dying
and there is no one else around."*

43.

she calls me on the telephone
wants to know
if I am home
wants to know
where I will go
and wants to know why words are cheap
and lies are easy

then she doesn't believe what I say
but a word to a word

a love to a no love
a relationship lived too long
a kiss hello
ultimately equals
a kiss goodbye

I sit here
2:35 A.M.
L.A. time
and she
is the only thing
left to write about

44.

I buy you gifts
because I love you
I buy you gifts
because you are me
I buy you gifts
because everything that I am
you have influenced
I buy you gifts
for all our years together
for all our years apart
for every reason
of no reason
and because my mind
hurts so much

I buy you gifts
because I love you
I buy you gifts
because I love myself
and the world keeps me
from loving you properly
it keeps me
from loving me properly
and from doing
what I truly want to do

I buy you gifts
so you will feel better
for I know
the world has taken its toll
on you as well

I buy you gifts
so I will feel better
buying them for you
is like someone
buying them for me

a dream
given to a dream

good night
sleep tight

45.

I roll over in bed
I call your name
I say,
"Come here, warm me up, I am cold."
I call for you
but my mind is somewhere else

my mind is with a dream
a vision that I saw today

I saw her
I loved her
I knew that she was the one

but she is there, out there
a dream
in a paved street
with chinese writing

you, you are here
though truthfully
I do not want you to be

have I traded
all the years of developing wisdom
all the years of desiring love
for you
the one I call
when there is no one else to call

your love it is killing me

46.

I show up
with lip stick on my collar
I show up for a date
with a love that has been lived too
long

lived to long
and has long been dead

I show up
with lip stick on my collar
from where
from whom
I do not even know
perhaps an angel
put it there
to free me
from the bounds
of love
lived too long

47.

I call her
for a fool's reason
I call her because
I have no one else to call

I call her
to scream
to yell at her
for keeping me around
when I never really wanted to be
together

I call her
to cry
for all that is missing
in my life
the life of a dreamer
chained to a world
wide awake
where life
is measured is time
and worth is counted
in dollars and cents

I call her
to tell her
I will never call her again
but we both know
that is a lie

48.

it is a hard reality to believe
it is an even harder one to face
to have known a lady
for more than six years
to have kissed her
to have made love with her
to have traveled with her
to have even lived with her
from time to time
but distance
from distant lands
and something always new on the horizon
has pulled us apart
or should I say
I have let it pull us apart

being together
was always being apart
for ours
was a half desired love
lived in half desired time
as the rationale of the world
continued on and on
as our desire
had us continue
to dance

but here it is
more than six years later
as I sit on the spot
which we first traveled to
and though I have the memory

and though I always long to be held
I have no desire
for the desire
the desire I once had for her

six years
wound in the spider's web
the web
the trap
filled with poison
venom of the snake
but I survived
walked out
into the air
of perpetual so called freedom
and now in my freedom
the spider finds its revenge
the revenge of hurt
from the distance
pain on the telephone lines
a bite of the knife
well, I've taken it before
so stab on

49.

I would call you
to tell you
good night
but you will not give me
your new telephone number
I would call you
but I can not
so once again
I go to bed alone
alone and in love
in love with with love
in love
with no one to love

I spend my days with you
my time
my money
all at my expense
I buy your time
I buy your presence
but your affection
you will no longer part with

you say
I have hurt you
too much
too many times
you say
that I have said it well
too much dirty water
under the bridge

I may have said it well
but I did not say it all
I did not tell you
that I do not need the chase

I need your love
your love
for one night more
for one year more
for one life time more
I did not say
that after six years
of our time together
that I still want to make love with you
I still need to know
your intimacies
to know
that you still
love me too
I never said
that we had to be together forever
forever
what a word
so short a time

you, you have touched no other
we both know
that I have
but touch
it often times means nothing

years and intimacy
mean so much more

and after all this time
I need to call you
say good night

I love you
for I have no one else
to tell it too

but you will not give me
your new telephone number
so I can say nothing
only write these useless words
on a page
that you will never see

50.

she told me
that she had no more tears
to cry over me
I said to her
come on
there must be a few more left

in the ages of spinning passion
the passion to run away
in the days
of fading glory
the clouds parted
to show the sun
that never was

embrace
disgrace
lies and love
and all the stories that could be told
Saturday nights
sitting home
watching T.V.
she is so far away

51.

her skin
it has become whiter
far more white
as age
has come upon us

I see the white
entering her skin
and I begin to cry

her face
has begun to show a line or two
lines
that were never there before

with every birth
there is an end
and all life
comes to a place
where there is
absolutely nothing left

it has been so many years
that I have known her
years
that have blown away
it has been so many years
and I know
that I could never love anyone
anymore

it the span
of birth to death
in the span
of meeting

of movement
of running away
in the span
so long
so short a time
I love her
so much that it hurts

I look into her spanish eyes
the color is the same
as they have always been
the feelings though
they have changed
we are so together
that we may never be apart
so together
so apart
the thought of her
brings a tear to my eyes

can it ever be any different
can it?
I do not know
but with all that is
all that was
I am left alone
writing these words

I look onto her face
her face
the reflection
of my own
and I see the years
they move forward
taking their toll
and I sit down and cry

there have been others
I have run to their arms
others
they are nothing
they mean nothing
in the deepest fathoms
of my heart
all I long for is her
though at times
I have told myself
that it is not so

love and age
no control
I see her
I love her
there would never be another
that would ever come close

love and age
I see her
I love her
again and again
we will never be apart

in her face
I can see the age
whiter
it has become far more white
and for her
I cry a tear
and maybe for myself as well
for if she is getting older
I am getting older
and neither one of us
has accomplished what
we set out to do

52.

when I knew her
she was a child

when I knew her
I was young

but the time
it has passed
and the visions of a child
which I once saw in her eyes
the visions of a child
which I once heard
spoken from her lips
have faded
they have become hardened
with the pursuits of the world
the world
that shows no mercy

when I knew her
she was young

when I knew her
I was young

youth it has faded
the lines
they have begun to appear
I am sure
that she never intended it that way
as I am sure
that I certainly never did

when you are young
you think you have forever
but the years
they have worsened us
they have hardened us
in their wisdom
they have tainted us
in what we have seen

I never meant it
to be that way
I am sure
neither did she

when I knew her
she was young

when I knew her
I was young

and now all that *is* left
all that is evident
is the passing
the fading glory
of youth expired
far too soon
used up
by the wasted world
and the relentless passing
of time

when I knew her
she was young

when I knew her
I was young

53.

was it so long ago
when we had the desire
to stop along
daytime
highway 101 north
between santa cruz and san francisco
and make love
for no reason but to make love

was it so long ago
when we took a moment
in the winter sierra nevada
to lay in the forest
and hold each other

was it so long ago
when we were chased
by dark green clouds
in the dark blue ocean night
as we ran across the sand

where did it go
why did we become so tainted

why did the world
come down so hard
on the both of us
so hard
that she
couldn't let her hair blow in the wind
so hard
that I had to fuck every woman possible

seeking
and looking

psychology
and pain
we have all
cried our tears

having
and not having
love
and lust
running
the running

where can I run to now
when she killed the all that I had left

54.

I wish there were days
that we could dream together again
dream of all that is
all that is to come
everything and the nothing

I wish there were days
that we could dream together again
drink cappuccino outside
have a late night
pie and coffee session
nowhere to be
and everything to see

I wish there were days
that we could dream together again
books to buy
love to make
money in the bank
time to kill and money to spill

I think of you

55.

I would call you from afar
if I had your telephone number
I would call you from afar
and ask you
to come back to me

afar
goes on forever and ever
where does it end
you and I
we both know the truth
but I need someone
I need to need someone
and you are the only one
who comes to mind

I would telephone you
in this late night
awake you from your sleep
I would telephone you
tell you that I love you
but I am sure
that you would just
hang up on me

56.

sometimes
you run
so far out
that you run in

sometimes
you try
so hard to leave
that you end up
with nothing at all

and where were you
when I needed you
while I was so alone

and where were you
when I was crying
you were nowhere
to be found

I danced in
too hard
I wanted out

it was my fault
in
it was my desire
out

age
it tempers the senses

life
it tempers the mind
love
turns into longing attachment

alone
it equals nothing at all
and if I had
another painting to paint
it would also
be inspired by you

and if I had another dream to live
you would be apart
of it too

I was there
when you were crying
but my tears
find no place to fall
I was there
when you had nobody
but me
I sit here all alone

forgive
and forget
seems to be the key to life
forgive
and forget them all

walking into the arms of nobody
driving the streets alone
living in longed for passion
makes you remember
what you had

and wonder
why you ran away

sure, I feel

57.

when will you have time to paint?
when will you have time to dream?

where does vision go

am I the last to be left with it
am I the last one
out here on the front lines
am I the last
refusing to give in
refusing to settle
for a life not filled with art

what about your going to graduate art
school?

where does vision go

a post card
in a p.o. box
I had been gone
out of her life
far too long
"I am a stewardess."
a waitress in the shy
by any other name

screaming for the dream
I was out
I was gone
asia, southeast asia
love

and lust
sex
and folly

home
I find a post card
stewardess
gone and away

let me tell you a story
a story of seven years ago
a story of a woman
who inspired my art
inspired my art
but was artistically frustrated herself

let me tell you about her
how I gave her a chance to dream
how she quit a secretary job
turned down one
to fly in the friendly sky
"That's too low for me."
"I don't want to be some one's
servant."
"I would never be a waitress."

time and life
and inspirations to dream
or not to dream
artist
that don't remain artist
like rimbau

artist
who buy the lie
take the jobs

and no longer have time
to create

I came back
I was gone a long time
I came back
and it was too late
to influence her to dream again

was it only I?
I, who held her to the art
I, who gave her the vision
I?

I do not feel a loss
such as loss
has been a major product of my life
I do not feel rejection
for years I tried to run away from her
what I feel is disappointment
as I have lost a battle to the world
once more

the world has won
shutting down an artist
shutting down a visionary
and robbing one more form of beauty

from the eyes of those
who have the eyes to see

my battle
has just become
one person harder

when will you have the time
to drink cappuccino out doors?

when will you have the space
to accomplish nothing at all?
when will you have days
when nothing really matters?
when will you have anything
anything but a job at all?

where does vision go
who steals it
and why

58.

oh well, goodbye
see you someday
when the ocean wind is blowing
      through your hair
and there is a twinkle in your eyes

oh well, goodbye
see you someday
when there is poetry in your words
and laughter in your voices

oh well, goodbye
see you someday
on a Tuesday morning
when the sun is shining
and the air is cool

oh well, goodbye
see you someday
when we are walking in the rain
and there is love in our hearts
and nothing but our moment matter at
all

oh well, goodbye

Scott Shaw Books-in-Print include:

About Peace: A 108 Ways to Be at Peace When Things Are Out of Control

Advanced Taekwondo

Apostrophe Zen

Arc Left from Istanbul

Ballet for a Funeral

Bangkok and the Nights of Drunken Stupor

Bangkok: Beyond the Buddha

Bus Ride(s)

Cairo: Before the Aftermath

Cambodian Refugees in Long Beach, California: The Definitive Study

Chi Kung for Beginners

China Deep

Echoes from Hell

Essence: The Zen of Everything

e.q.

Guangzhou: A Photographic Exploration

Hapkido: Articles on Self-Defense: Volume 1

Hapkido: Articles on Self-Defense: Volume 2

Hapkido: Essays on Self-Defense

Hapkido: The Korean Art of Self-Defense

Hong Kong: Out of Focus

Independent Filmmaking: Secrets of the Craft

In the Foreboding Shadows of Holiness

Israel in the Oblique

Junk: The Backstreets of Bangkok

Katmandu and Beyond: A Photographic Exploration

Last Will and Testament According to the

Divine Rites of the Drug Cocaine

L.A. Street Shots: A Photographic Exploration

L.A.: Tales from the Suburban Side of Hell

Los Angeles Skidrow: 1983

Marguerite Duras and Charles Bukowski: The Yin and Yang of Modern Erotic Literature

Mastering Health: The A to Z of Chi Kung

Nirvana in a Nutshell

One Word Meditations

On the Hard Edge of Hollywood

Pagan, Burma: Shadows of the Stupa

Rangoon and Mandalay: A Photographic Exploration

Sake' in a Glass, Sushi with Your Fingers: Fifteen Minutes in Tokyo

Scream of the Buddha

Scream: Southeast Asia and the Dream

Scribbles on the Restroom Wall

Samurai Zen

Sedona: Realm of the Vortex

Shama Baba

Shanghai Whispers Shanghai Screams

Shattered Thoughts

Singaore: Off Center

South Korea in a Blur

Suicide Slowly

Taekwondo Basics

Ten to Thirty

The Abstract Arsenal of Zen and the Psychology of Being

The Chronicles: Zen Ramblings from the Internet

The Ki Process: Korean Secrets for Cultivating Dynamic Energy

The Little Book of Yoga Breathing

The Little Book of Zen Mediation

The Lyrics

The Most Beautiful Woman in Shanghai

The Passionate Kiss of Illusion

The Screenplays

The Tao of Chi

The Tao of Self Defense

The Voodoo Buddha

The Warrior is Silent: Martial Arts and the Spiritual Path

The Zen of Life, Lies, and Aberrant Reality

The Zen of Modern Life and the Reality of Reality

TKO: Lost Nights in Tokyo

Urban India: Bombay, Delhi, Lucknow

Varanasi and Bodhi Gaya: Shades of the Bodhi Tree

Wet Dreams and Placid Silence

Woods in the Wind

Yoga: A Spiritual Guidebook

Yosemite: End of the Winter

Zen and Modern Consciousness

Zen Buddhism: The Pathway to Nirvana

Zen Filmmaking

Zen Filmmaking 2: Further Writing on the Cinematic Arts

Zen Mind Life Thoughts

Zen in the Blink of an Eye

Zen Mind Life Thought

Zen O'clock: Time to Be

Zen: Tales from the Journey
Zero One